Preparing for the Next Great Recession

How to Not Let the Sudden Economic Downturn Catch You by Surprise

By: Emily Watson

9781681279442

PUBLISHERS NOTES

Disclaimer – Speedy Publishing LLC

This publication is intended to provide helpful and informative material. It is not intended to diagnose, treat, cure, or prevent any health problem or condition, nor is intended to replace the advice of a physician. No action should be taken solely on the contents of this book. Always consult your physician or qualified health-care professional on any matters regarding your health and before adopting any suggestions in this book or drawing inferences from it.

The author and publisher specifically disclaim all responsibility for any liability, loss or risk, personal or otherwise, which is incurred as a consequence, directly or indirectly, from the use or application of any contents of this book.

Any and all product names referenced within this book are the trademarks of their respective owners. None of these owners have sponsored, authorized, endorsed, or approved this book.

Always read all information provided by the manufacturers' product labels before using their products. The author and publisher are not responsible for claims made by manufacturers.

This book was originally printed before 2014. This is an adapted reprint by Speedy Publishing LLC with newly updated content designed to help readers with much more accurate and timely information and data.

Speedy Publishing LLC

40 E Main Street, Newark, Delaware, 19711

Contact Us: 1-888-248-4521

Website: http://www.speedypublishing.co

REPRINTED Paperback Edition: 9781681279442:

Manufactured in the United States of America

DEDICATION

This book is dedicated to my boss, Angela. Thank you for believing in me and for allowing me to blossom as a writer.

TABLE OF CONTENTS

Chapter 1- The Instability of the Economy and How It Affects You.. 5

Chapter 2- How to Stay Out of Debt.. 9

Chapter 3- Save for an Economic Crunch Time 14

Chapter 4- Protect Your Business 18

Chapter 5- How to Save on the Usual Expenses 21

Chapter 6 – Be Your Own Seller 33

Chapter 7 – Is It Time to Try a New Career?.........................36

Chapter 8 – What Investments are Safe from Recession?............41

Chapter 9 – How to Bring More Sales to Your Business during Recession..44

About The Author..47

Chapter 1 - The Instability of the Economy and How It Affects You

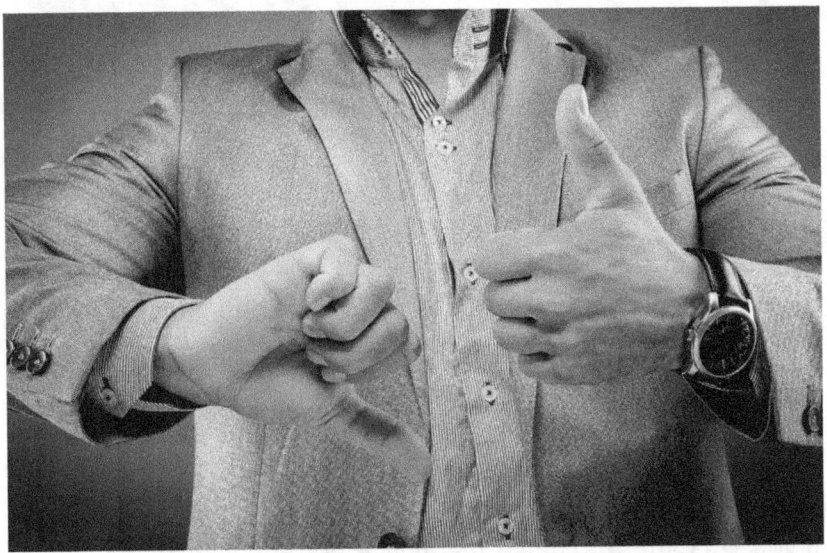

Are you like many of us, concerning yourself about the economic system, sky skyrocketing fuel prices and the cost of just living? Regrettably, these are matters that we have to consider nowadays. Over the preceding year, particularly, we have experienced the prices of day-to-day items skyrocket. Read on for a few helpful tips that can assist you in learning to save income. They're amazingly easy. We can easily miss them; but they may have a huge effect on our budget.

In this time of economical adversity, we need to be motivated to make the most of what we have acquired.

The current universal recession has seen a lot of people finding it difficult to preserve their lush life-styles. To a few individuals it's become even hard to fulfill their day-to-day necessities. Matters that earlier were needs have now gotten to be wants since they're no more affordable and somebody has no alternative but to live without them, all ascribable to the economic recession.

Preparing for the Next Great Recession

It's consequently become imperative for individuals to discover ways to pass through from this lush lifestyle smoothly in order, to the lowest degree, meet the primary essentials of life. It may prove to be rather a project particularly where youngsters are affected, they might not comprehend why matters have changed drastically therefore as a parent you need to explain to them precisely what is coming about.

A point to look at would be if you used to go to the local movie theater for movies every now and then, you are able to choose to go to the video store and choose some up to date movies, whip up a few snacks to crunch on as you view the movies in the house. As for those who previously go for extended holidays as international tourist However now they can't afford to do the same, they may decide to be local tourist.

If you can't afford to buy something at present, instead of straining yourself it might be advisable to begin saving for it. The additional matter to avoid is acquiring a charge card that you can't afford to pay for. Charge cards are a venomous circle where if you're not heedful you'll be just paying the interest therefore it can destroy your monetary resources. Consequently, prevent the use of charge plates and purchase just what you are able to afford for today as you wait for the economic system and your financial condition to stabilize.

Everybody can use a bit of additional room in their budget. You might be worried about climbing gas prices and its result on the price of your groceries and so forth. Well, never fear as I'm here are some techniques that you are able to do today to help you save as well as make some money in these hard times.

Emily Watson
The Debt and Recession Relationship

Let me tell you from experience, discounting your debt issue are only going to produce more unimaginable issues down the road, which won't be so pleasant for you. Any debts that go unpaid for very long will finally all catch up to you and because of waiting as you did, your credit rating, as well as your good responsible standing with a few creditors, will simply be completely ruined and add to the ills of the recession.

Nobody wishes to think about losing all of their precious possessions but let me tell you, if you carry on ignoring your debt condition, it may happen to you. If you don't pay your creditors, your assets may and will eventually be removed from you, one way or another and I do know that none of us really want or anticipate that sort of thing occurring right?

The best advice I may possibly give to you all, when it comes to easing some of that horrid debt, would be to take action now, before it is too late! You do have numerous options when it comes to getting rid of some of that debt that has been simply piling up on you and ways to fight the recession. However nothing will take place unless you're prepared to take action and make it happen, so make certain you keep that in mind ok!

Debt relief may be something as little as following an appropriate budget, rather than spending money that you truly may not afford to spend anyway. Make your life a little bit simpler by doing something to get rid of that debt that's simply going to keep getting worse and worse if you continue down the path you're presently traveling.

Don't let your debt issue get in the way and prevent you from enjoying life the way that you ought to be enjoying it, to the fullest,

Preparing for the Next Great Recession
without so much stress happening daily! Get back the command over your life that you once had, it's up to you because nobody else out there is going to mend things for you!

Chapter 2- How to Stay Out of Debt

Too much debt is what too many of you know about correct? Yes, debt may be a killer if it comes to attempting to make it financially, in this hard world that we live in.

Arriving at smart choices and being knowledgeable about earning cash, saving cash, investing cash and not getting into too much debt, are crucial issues of interest that ought to be noticed much more than they are by many.

Throughout this article I want to discuss with you all some helpful information that could potentially help to prevent you from getting into too much debt early on in your adult life story. A lot of people who are simply coming out of high school or college often make the same mistake, they rush right into to a lot of different things that they may not afford to pay for, so they finance or charge it all!

Doing this is what begins this terrible and occasionally painful cycle that is not going to do anything except cause you strain and

Preparing for the Next Great Recession

struggle all throughout life. Knowing and comprehending simply how serious of an issue this may be is very crucial and finding out this sort of stuff early on in life may really be really helpful and may save you a good deal of heartache later on in life, if you're working on paying off a lot of your debts that you've collected over the years, for one thing or another.

Debt may ruin any person's life story, so no matter how much cash you have or don't have, be cognizant that without even recognizing it quickly enough, debt may start piling up, and start eating you alive.

It is not something that a lot of us ever plan on having to deal with but regrettably throughout life, a few things do tend to occur that we simply may not control and often times that unfortunate incident may cost you a substantial amount of cash, cash that you or nobody else may ever truly afford.

It is so really important for everybody to understand early on in life story simply how hard your adulthood may be because of uncontrollably rising debts every month.

This is why you ought to be always be cognizant of the fact that it may indeed happen to you, simply as with anyone else that you know and if you're cognizant of all the risks surrounding you then you ought to be most definitely be more prepared in knowing simply what to do if and if that time does ever come for you, at any unforeseen moment throughout the duration of your life story.

Don't let debt be your controller, you control all of your actions and try and be as responsible as ever, whenever it comes to how much and what you choose to spend your hard earned cash on.

Emily Watson

Knowledge of your financial standing at all times, along with some great judgment, if it comes to spending those finances, will help to ensure that debt crisis's will never be a part of your life story.

Develop Your Budgeting Skills

Getting a budget may not sound like the most exciting matter in the world to do, but it's vital in keeping your finances in order and betting the recession. Before you begin to produce your budget it's important to recognize that in order to be successful you have to supply as much detailed info as possible. Finally, the end result will show where your money is coming from, how much is there and where it's all being spent.

Accumulate every financial statement you are able to.

This includes bank statements, investing account statements, current public utility bills and whatsoever info concerning a source of money or disbursement. The operative for this action is to produce a monthly average so the more info you are able to turn up the better.

Look at all of your origins of money.

If you're self-employed or have any exterior sources of money make certain to put down these also. If your money is in the form of a steady payroll check where taxes are mechanically withheld then using the net income, or brings home pay, amount is all right. Put down this entire money as a monthly sum.

Produce a list of monthly disbursals.

Put down a list of all the anticipated disbursals you plan on receiving over the course of a calendar month. This includes a mortgage defrayment, car defrayments, auto policy, grocery store, public utilities, amusement, dry cleaning, car insurance, retirement or college nest egg and basically everything you spend money on.

Break up disbursals into 2 classes: fixed and varying. Fixed disbursals are those that remain comparatively the same monthly and are demanded parts of your way of living. They included disbursals like your mortgage or rent, auto defrayments, cable and/or net service, garbage collection, charge card payments and so forth. These disbursals for the most part are necessary yet not likely to alter in the budget.

Varying disbursals are the type that will alter from month to month and include items like groceries, gas, amusement, dining out and gifts to name some. This class will be crucial when making changes.

Tally your monthly income and monthly disbursals.

If your end resultant shows more money than disbursals you're off to a beneficial beginning. This means you are able to prioritize this surplus to areas of your budget like retirement savings or paying more on charge cards to wipe out that debt quicker. If you're showing a higher disbursement column than money it means some changes will have to be established.

Establish changes to disbursals.

If you have precisely described and listed all of your expenses the elemental goal would be to have your money and disbursement columns to match. This means all of your money is calculated for and budgeted for a particular disbursement.

If you're in a state of affairs where disbursals are greater than money you should view your variable disbursals to determine areas to cut down. Since these disbursals are usually not necessary it should be easy to shave a couple of dollars in a couple of areas to bring you closer to your money.

Go over your budget every month.

It's crucial to reexamine your budget on a steady basis to make sure you're remaining on track. After the 1st month take a minute to sit down and equate the actual disbursals versus what you had acquired in the budget. This will show you where you handled best and where you may need to improve.

Chapter 3 - Save for an Economic Crunch Time

In this economic crunch time you really need to learn how to save some money. Here are some tips.

Food is amidst the biggest expenses, along with housing and cars, in most folk's budget. If you're seeking ways to cut down on your budget, your food should be one thing you view closely - there's almost always ways to cut down here. 1st, dine out to a lesser extent and fix your own food - this will save heaps of cash. However shop sagely.

- Make a weekly menu. Make certain to plan a leftovers night.

- Always go with a list. Now stick to that list - don't buy anything not on the list.

- Get a budget. If you go to shop, know exactly how much you are able to spend. Keep a running score as you shop to check that you're inside your budget.

- Don't go if you are hungry. You'll wind up spending a lot more. Consume a good meal first, and you'll be more probable to adhere to your list.

- Check your pantry and keep a list. Put a stroke next to each item for the number of items you have. Then, cross off what you use. This makes it much simpler if it comes time to make your list.

- Retain your receipts, and then put down into a spreadsheet. This will be your cost list. Utilize it so you know if mass or sale items are a beneficial deal.

- Purchase frozen veggies. Since you're able to keep them in the deep freezer, they rarely spoil.

- Cut back meat. Meat is expensive. Design vegetarian meals many times a week and for additional meals.

- Look for specials. Every shop has specials. Make sure to look for them in the paper, or if you get to the store.

- Use store discount cards. These may add together to bring huge savings over the long haul.

- Consume water. It's a great deal better for you, and a great deal cheaper.

If it comes to preserving cash on your electric bill, people from one coast to the other recognize the big ones: suitable insulation, water conservation and lowering the thermostat may lead to major long-run power savings, but there are a great deal of little recognized things you're able to do around the home that may lead to substantial savings, besides.

Preparing for the Next Great Recession

- We all recognize that the greatest power pig in the normal house is the washer and dryer. You're able to significantly cut down the amount of power you utilize if you upgrade your machines to newer, EnergyStar endorsed ones, but if that is not in the budget, try throwing in a couple of dry face towels into your next wet dryer load. You're able to cut down each dryer load by as much as 20 minutes with the inclusion of two simple dry face cloths.

- Do not utilize the heat dry alternative on your dishwasher.

- Heat drying is entirely unneeded and many newer models don't even have the choice for it any longer. By merely cutting off this one frivolous process, you're able to start to save money on electrical power almost immediately.

- Use cold water. If you truly prefer to save cash on electrical power, wash all of your garments on cold, including your whites, and merely run one cycle a month on hot with whitener to keep your whites vivid.

- Ask about a free power inspection. Your local power company may provide the best free power preserving program of all. Depending upon which electric company you have, you might measure up for a free assessment of your house by a power authority.

Let's take a look at assorted wise moves you are able to take to save on entertainment costs without cutting off the fun:

- Heading to the theater if matinees are being displayed may save you 2 or 3 dollars off of the cost of a ticket. Even better, is to wait till the movie appears on tape and pay $four for a movie rental. Better: snag the movie from your public library where it's either free or will cost you a nominal fee.

Emily Watson

- Get the discount - Zoos, parks, museums, galleries and additional public locales commonly have leastwise one day per week where you and your loved ones may get allowed in for a discount. Check into their site to seek specials.

- Accompany a group - Your big family may not qualify for a group grade, but if you've friends and neighbors who are interested in visiting the same theme park or would like to see the same show at the amphitheater, you might ask for a price reduction.

- Use memberships - individuals who are members of AARP, AAA, or another big and long-familiar association are frequently extended price reductions if they flaunt their card. Professional affiliations may occasionally bring savings your way likewise, so before you book your next room, do a car rental, or consider a flight, determine which card works for you.

- Find gratis events - passing time at a public park, going to your local college campus for a public event, or seeing a state run art museum typically means one thing: your time there is free.

CHAPTER 4- PROTECT YOUR BUSINESS

Regrettably for you, you're not AIG and you're not qualified for a ceaseless line of life from the United States. If a company of that magnitude came down, it will for certain be felt around the globe. However you? You're just a little business owner and you're, in every feel of the word, little. Don't be concerned however. It's possible to outride this recession with your business still in good shape. Read on for additional info.

Hint # 1: Observe what you're paying out.

At present, to a higher degree than ever, is the time for you to scrutinize your expenditures. And that's from your bond paper to your public utility accounts. How much are they costing you per calendar month? Are you returning any waste by allowing for the lights to be left on? Are you keeping up your equipment correctly avoiding crazily big repair expenditures?

Emily Watson
Hint # 2: Reduce your expenditures.

After observing of your expenditures, you have to cut back on them. You need to scrutinize for your small business costs is to discover where you are able to save up. If you're outlay a bit much on tissue paper, cut back on usage. Be watchful. Perpetually seek directions to bring down costs and to optimize. You'd be amazed at how small deletions bestow huge savings.

Hint #3: Let go employees only you have to.

Wages absorb a chunk of small business expenditures, However keep in mind that it will cost you a great deal more if you do everything yourself. What's more is the reality that it might be damaging to your small business if you substitute existing employees with naïve new hires. I know of a real estate assessment company, who didn't mind their talent and son, they're suffering at present. Knowledgeable employees are by nature more expensive. However don't forget that they're also more effective. If you are sailing fierce seas because of the economic system, keep your employees in the loop! They'd value it. They might even go the additional mile for you. Remember, no one prefers to turn a loss on their job in this economic system either.

Hint #4: Let go clients who are not worth it.

Oh thigh-slapper. I can't begin discussing this and not just continue on and on and on. There are simply merely customers who are not worth maintaining. They're normally the ones who bargain for the bottom price but are the hardest. Since I'm in the service industry, I just merely jack up my cost to fire them. And I cite the sort of service that they require as the reason for the fresh price. Don't let your customers to step all over you just because it's a recession. Time is as well income. And time exhausted on customers who are overly difficult might be better spent on promoting your small business to draw in the type of customers that you'd like to service.

Hint #5: Discover your niche.

Observe where the absolute majority of your business is faring from. Are they from old persons? Working mommies? If you discover your niche, it's easier to yield more business in that certain demographic. Over the long-run, you'll find that proceeding within your niche in reality makes you more fruitful for a lot less efforts.

Hint #6: Expand your promotion endeavors.

During hard times, the budget for promotion and advertising is frequently the first one to be trounced. No, nah, nay. Never do that. A recession is all the more cause that you should proceed in your promotion efforts for your small business. Individuals will still keep purchasing even during recession, and they're more likely to only purchase the brands they know. Where are your challengers now? Are they hiding out? Grab this chance to make yourself well-known. When the recession is all over, you'll find your small business leading the market.

Hint #7: Remain confident.

It's difficult to break a smile when everybody is busy whirling of fresh story of gloominess and doomsday because of the economic system. But stay confident, all right? If you want your small business to remain afloat, don't shape your mind to fail. Be pleased even during unsure times. Remember, a recession is simply an impermanent condition. If there's a break, there will also be a blast. While you're ready and waiting, keep yourself and your small business united by remaining confident despite everything.

Chapter 5- How to Save on the Usual Expenses

- **Fuel**

1. Ease Up

Among the better ways to save fuel is to plainly reduce your speed. As speed step-ups, gas economy lessens exponentially. If you're among the "ten-over on the expressway" set, attempt driving the speed limit for a couple of days. You'll save more fuel and your travel won't take much longer. (Just make sure you stay to the right, so you won't block the less-enlightened.)

Preparing for the Next Great Recession

2. Ascertain your tire pressure

Under-inflated tires are among the many commonly brushed off causes of cheesy MPG. Tires mislay air due to age and temperature; under-inflated tires have more rolling impedance, which means you require burning more fuel to keep your car running. Purchase a dependable tire gauge and check your tires at least once a month. Make certain to check them when they're frigid, since driving the car warms the tires along with the air within them, which step-ups pressure and gives an incorrectly elevated reading. Utilize the inflation pressures shown in the owner's manual or on the information plate in the driver's doorpost.

3. Scope out your air cleaner

A dirty air cleaner confines the airflow into the engine, which damages performance and saving. Air cleaners are simple to check and alter; take out the filter and hold it up to the sun. If you can't see light breaking through it, you need a fresh one.

4. Speed up with caution

Jack-rabbit beginnings are a visible fuel-waster -- but that doesn't mean you ought to crawl away from every light. If you have an automatic, speed up with moderation so the transmission can shift up into the greater gears. Stick-shifters ought to shift ahead of time to keep the revs down, but do not lug the engine -- downshift if you want to accelerate. Keep an eye well down the road for likely slowdowns. If you speed up to speed then have to brake directly, that's diminished fuel.

Emily Watson

5. Stay with the trucks

Ever observe how, in foul snarl-ups, autos seem to perpetually accelerate and decelerate, while trucks tend to roll along at the same easygoing pace? A ceaseless speed keeps shifting to a minimal -- crucial to those who have to haggle with those ten-speed truck transmissions -- but it as well helps thriftiness, as it takes much more gas to get a vehicle propelling than it does to keep it propelling. Rolling with the big trucks economizes gas.

6. Return to nature

Think about shutting off the air conditioning, opening the windows and delighting in the breeze. It might be a shade warmer, However at lower speeds you'll economize gas. That said, at greater speeds the A/C might be more effective than the wind opposition from open windows and sunroof. If I'm going somewhere where making it sweaty and smelly may be an issue, I bring an additional shirt and leave ahead of time so I'll have time for a prompt change.

7. Back down from the bling-bling

New wheels and tires may appear cool, and they may surely improve handling. But if they're wider than the stock tires, chances are they'll produce more rolling impedance and diminish gas saving. If you upgrade your wheels and tires, hold on to the old ones.

8. Clear out your auto

If you're the character who takes an easygoing attitude towards auto cleanliness -- sporadically go through your auto and see what can be cast away or brought into the house. It doesn't take much to gain an extra forty or fifty lbs. of stuff and the additional weight your car has to tote around, the more gas it burns.

9. Go smaller

If you're shopping for a fresh auto, it's time to reassess how much automobile you truly require. Littler cars are inherently more fuel-efficient, and today's little autos are more spacious than ever. Concerned about wreck protection? The auto manufacturers are planning their little cars to survive wrecks with larger vehicles, and safety features like side-curtain airbags and electronic stableness control are becoming old-hat in littler cars.

10. Don't use a car

Not a popular matter, I know, but the reality is that if you are able to prevent driving, you'll save fuel. Take the train, carpool, and consolidate your buying trips. Walking or bicycling is beneficial for your wallet and your wellness. And before you go into your auto, always ask yourself: "Is this trip truly essential?"

- **Electric Bills**

Your washing machine and dryer are big energy pigs!

We all recognize that the greatest energy pig in the normal house is the washing machine and dryer. You are able to significantly cut down the amount of energy you utilize if you upgrade your machines to newer, EnergyStar endorsed ones, but if that Is not in the budget, try throwing in a couple of dry face towels into your next wet dryer load. Analyses have shown you are able to cut down each dryer load by as much as twenty minutes with the inclusion of two simple dry face cloths. If you do not have an energy effective dryer, this will assist you in saving money on electrical energy at once.

Do not utilize the heat dry alternative on your dishwashing machine.

The dishwashing machine has become an essential part of the house, but if you're utilizing the heat dry choice on your machine, you're wasting a huge amount of money. By utilizing a product like Jet Dry, you are able to merely open the door to your dishwashing machine and let your dishes air dry without spots taking shape on your glasses. Heat drying is entirely unneeded and many newer models don't even have the choice for it anymore. By merely cutting off this one frivolous process, you are able to start to save money on electrical energy almost immediately.

Clean your garments in cold water.

If you're among those individuals that always reads the labels on your garments, you already recognize that, for the most part, darks want to be washed out in cold water. According to many clothing industries, only white loads that have no black clothes in them in the least should be washed out on hot. If you truly prefer to save money on electrical energy, wash all of your garments on cold, including your whites, and merely run one cycle a month on hot with whitener to keep your whites vivid. If the entire globe stopped washing out clothes with hot water, we could save 1000000000000s of dollars a year in energy consumptions.

Inquire about a gratis energy inspection.

Lastly, your local energy company might provide the best free energy preserving program of all. Depending upon which electric company you have, you might measure up for a free assessment of

Preparing for the Next Great Recession

your house by an energy authority. A spokesperson of your electric company can visit your house and walk you through the assorted places in which you're leaking power. In many cases, the answers are very easy and you are able to save money on electrical energy straight off. Get hold of your electric company today to see if this service is available in your area.

- Groceries

1. Design out an every week menu. This is the finest way to assure that your list is complete, and that you've plenty to serve your family dinner for the week. You are able to plan a weekly menu then duplicate it for the following week — this way you are able to shop for 2 weeks at a time. Make sure to plan a leftovers night.

2. Forever go with a list. If you go without a list, you might as well simply throw your income aside. Develop a list of everything you require, making a point you have everything required for your weekly menu and checking to make certain you don't hold it in your pantry, fridge or deep freezer. Make certain you're not blanking out anything. Now adhere to that list - don't purchase anything not on the list.

3. Get a budget. When you go to shop, know precisely how much you are able to spend. Then attempt your best to stick inside that boundary. If you don't recognize how much you are able to spend, you'll for sure spend a bit much. Maintain a running score as you shop to ascertain that you're inside your budget.

4. Do not go when you are hungry. This is a basic tip, but it's reliable - when you're hungry, you would like to buy all sorts of junk. You'll wind up spending a lot more. Consume a good meal first, and you'll be more probable to adhere to your list.

Emily Watson

5. Check your pantry. Attain a checklist of everything you commonly stock in your pantry. Keep it placed on the pantry. Put a stroke next to each item for the number of items you have. Then, when you utilize something, convert the slash into an X. This makes it much simpler when it comes time to arrive at your list.

6. Retain your receipts, and then put down into a spreadsheet. This will be your cost list. Utilize it so you know when mass or sale items are a beneficial deal. It's likewise a bang-up way to comparison shop between shops. The spreadsheet may likewise serve as a checklist to utilize when you're composing your grocery list.

7. Purchase frozen vegetables. While fresh vegetables are a little more beneficial, frozen vegetables are almost as beneficial, as and much better than zip. And since you are able to keep them in the deep freezer, they rarely spoil.

8. Reduce meat. Meat is expensive. Design vegetarian meals many times a week and for additional meals, you may just utilize a little meat as a sort of seasoning rather than the chief ingredient.

9. Fix a great deal, and then freeze. Design to cook a huge amount of food and freeze it for multiple dinners. A bang-up idea is to utilize one Sunday and cook a week's worth of dinners.

10. Seek specials. Every shop has specials. Make sure to seek them in the paper, or when you get to the store. Don't purchase them unless they're things you forever use.

11. Sample the store brands. Trade names are frequently no better than generic, and you're compensating for all the advertising they do to have a trade name. Give the store brand a sample,

and frequently you won't observe a difference. Particularly if it's an element in a dish where you can't taste the caliber of that separate ingredient

12. Trim down on your "one-item" trips. They waste fuel, and almost unavoidably, you purchase more than that one item. If you project ahead, make a weekly menu, and shop with a list, this ought to drastically cut down the number of trips you make for a little number of items. However if you still discover yourself running out for a couple of items, break down the reason — are you not establishing a beneficial list, are you blanking out a few items from your list? Prevent trips to the convenience store. Or the filling station! These are a few of the most expensive stores.

13. Utilize store discount cards. These can add together to bring huge savings over the long haul.

14. Consume water. If you on a regular basis drink ice tea, Kool-Aid, pops or other forms of drinks, cut those out totally and just drink water. It's a great deal better for you, and a great deal cheaper.

- Fun Time and Gimmick

A Disorderly securities market has many individuals concerned and for good reason: no one is rather sure what the effect of these movements will be. Given that a fresh president and Congress are running the country, consumers have more causes to question what the future holds for them.

However, life continues and we can't let issues that we have no control over order our lives. We need to go on subsisting and among the ways we savor our lives is by amusement pastimes. As you recognize, amusement can absorb a substantial chunk of your budget and is frequently the first thing that gets reduced when the economic system turns.

Luckily, there are methods for you to all the same savor a movie, an afternoon performing putt-putt with the children, or even take a family holiday without breaking your budget. Let's take a look at various wise moves you are able to take to save on amusement costs without cutting off the fun:

View a movie — maneuvering to the theater when matinees are being displayed can save you 2 or 3 dollars off of the cost of a ticket. Even finer, is to wait till the movie appears on tape and pay $four for a movie rental. Better: snag the movie from your public library where it's either free or will cost you a token fee.

Acquire the price reduction — Zoos, parks, museums, galleries and additional public locales commonly have leastwise one day per week where you and your loved ones can get allowed in for a discount. Check into their site to seek specials which might include a printable price reduction coupon. A few of the bigger regional theme parks print their discount rate on locally bottled cans of your preferred soft drink or snack.

Accompany a group — your big family might not qualify for a group grade, but if you've friends and neighbors who are interested in visiting the same theme park or would like to see the same show at the amphitheater, you may ask for a price reduction. Send a big enough groups to a ball game and your group may be picked out on the home team's scoreboard!

Utilize memberships — individuals who are members of AARP, AAA, or another big and long-familiar association are frequently extended price reductions when they flaunt their card. Professional affiliations may occasionally bring savings your way likewise, so

Preparing for the Next Great Recession

before you book your next room, do a car rental, or consider a flight, determine which card works for you.

Eleventh hour planning — projecting ahead can generate bountiful deductions, but so can waiting till the eleventh hour, particularly if you're elastic with your plans. Having young tykes in tow can make this hard to do, but if you're seeking a discount on a flight, some airways will give to you their better price if you're at the airport and willing to fly standby. Hotels prefer to fill beds while theaters will frequently cut ticket prices at the eleventh hour.

Discover gratis events – passing time at a public park, maneuvering to your local college campus for a public event, or seeing a state run art museum typically means one thing: your time there is gratis. In a few cases you'll pay a token fee to enjoy a college demonstration, which can be rather good, but with free parking available, you'll discover the savings to tote up compared to a night out on the town.

Your weekly residential area papers can be a trove of fantabulous info on free or discounted events in your area. Several are gratis and a few provide prizes, one more bonus to bring your kinsperson to a fun event.

• Taxes

When it bears on saving taxes, being proactive is by all odds the way to go. Take a fresh view of ways to preserve money. Here are a few hints to assist you:

1. Where are you distributing income?

Where do you distribute income every month? Something I advocate to everybody is to consider t their monthly disbursements every now and then and ascertain what can be moved from the personal side to the business side.

Remember, to make a disbursement a lawful write-off you need to ask yourself if that disbursement passes the "reasonable and essential for the output of revenue" test.

Take cellular phones, for instance. Do you utilize a cellular phone to touch base with your customers or clients? Then the expenditures to operate that mobile phone are a lawful business tax deduction.

As soon as I state that, somebody nearly always asks me about utilizing a cellular phone for both business and personal calls, and whether the expenditures should be apportioned accordingly. And while you may do this, I'm not always positive it's essential.

Most modernistic cell phone programs consist of a set number of minutes that you pay for irrespective of whether you use them or not. As long as you're not getting overage charges for personal calls, I would not be too worried.

For the Internal Revenue Service to ascertain whether your phone was being used more for joy than business, they'd have to examine your cellular phone records, call by call.

2. Doing estimated tax payments a matter of past times.

I don't know about you, but as a business owner drawing in earnings, I detest the thought that I might also be compelled to make extra tax payments. To me, that's one of the advantages to operating through a business.

If you're running as a Sole Proprietor (i.e., a Schedule C business), then you recognize all about approximated tax payments. Based on the former year's income tax return, the IRS determines how much tax you should pay the following year, and 4 times a year you get to issue a pretty big check.

3. Prevent paying late-payment punishments.

So if you file for an extension, you won't start making approximated tax payments till well into the next year--meaning that when the IRS processes your return and forecasts your estimated tax payments, they'll likewise add in punishments for late defrayal!

Well, here's a way to prevent all of that. You are able to prevent those punishments by making a supplemental tax withholding on your final December payroll check. Merely take a look at what you've claimed in profit draws this year and estimate the rough amount of income tax due on that total. Then, deduct that total from your final December payroll check.

If you are able to show the IRS that you've paid almost or all of your previous year's taxes inside that same tax year, you'll stand a really good chance of nullifying estimated tax payments completely. And that means you are able to say so long to those late-payment penalties, likewise!

4. Bringing in revenue in the most tax-advantaged way

Are you bringing in revenue in the most tax-advantaged way? It's truly easy to get caught in this snare and pay for more taxes than you need to by utilizing the wrong (or no) business structure. Even if you're speaking to a professional, if they don't ask the correct questions, and you don't offer the correct info, you could end up in an entity that does not fit your business.

Chapter 6 – Be Your Own Seller

To begin with, let's view some of the rationalities why you might choose to sell your home without a real estate agent:

- You have not owned the home that you're marketing for very long. In many cases, owning a house for only a short time period means that your equity in the home is depressed. The lower the equity, the more a real estate agent commissioning will gash into any earnings that you may realize from the sale of the home. If the sale won't profit you enough to pay the Realtor's commission, selling without a real estate agent is your most beneficial choice.

- You have the revenue up front for publicizing and listing costs. Without a real estate agent, you will be responsible for promoting your house for sale. These expenditures will include newspaper advertisements, printing expenditures for flyers, listing expenditures with Internet FSBO web sites and the price of signs to draw in purchasers. While this commonly bumps into hundreds of dollars, it is still a good deal less than the commission you'd pay a real estate agent.

- You have the time and accessibility to take calls from prospective purchasers and show your home. Plan to be available to accept telephone calls concerning your property for sale at all times of day, and schedule tours at times that are convenient for prospective purchasers - and not necessarily you! A compromising schedule will make it far easier to show your home and get it sold fast.

Generally, a homeowner who decides to sell without a real estate agent will spend between 2% and 3% of the eventual selling price of the home on sales-related disbursements. Presentation is everything! House purchasers are pulled in to clean, spacious and attractive homes. Your goal is to bedazzle purchasers. Brighten-up the home and remove all jumbles from counter tops, tables and rooms. Scrub-down your home from top to bottom. Make it glitter. Simple aesthetical improvements like cutting back trees, setting flowers, doctoring squeaking steps, broken tiles, shampooing rugs and even re-painting a washed-out bedroom will greatly heighten the appeal of your home. Likewise, make certain your house smells good. That's correct, clean out the kitty box and light gently scented candles.

Your ad copy should be thorough yet curt, easy and pertinent. Long, ornate prose won't make your home sound more likable. It will merely make it tougher for the house buyer to read. Make certain to supply the vital facts buyers are seeking like the house's number of baths, a remodeled kitchen, and so forth.

Emily Watson
Many home purchasers rapidly scan ads, so it's crucial that your house jumps out. For instance, you might want to add a theme-line like "Priced below market" or "bang-up schools." Remain away from business slang and use language that makes home purchasers comfy.

Chapter 7 – Is It Time to Try a New Career?

Seeking a line of work or believe you may be soon? Start recession-proofing your vocation by recession-proofing yourself. There are matters you are able to do to protect yourself in case the recession affects your company and your work. Begin now - don't wait till you discovery yourself discharged or differently unemployed.

- Promote and network - web logs or blogs are a great way to share who you are and what you do. You are able to raise your professional visibility by interacting and associating online. Get yourself recognized, so if the worst occurs, time in between careers will be less. Blogging is a great way to draw in fresh occupation opportunities. So, a lot of times it's not what you know, but instead, who you know? You are able to even begin a blog in order to get income directly.

- Bit-by-bit start produce secondary income - start freelancing. Begin a half-time business. Business owners usually have more than one customer, which helps recession-proof their operation. Consequently, if your full-time occupation and/or salary goes away, you are able to help "soften the blow" by transitioning your part-time independent business into fulltime employment (at least till you are able to secure another line of work with benefits).

- Make sure your prospective part-time freelancing (business) doesn't infringe on your daily work and your employer's conflict-of-interest policies.

- Produce your own site and provide consulting services or particular products.

- Begin a net business. Over time this may become more fruitful than your day occupation. There are many net marketers who bring in 6- figure-incomes or more, a few who make 1000000s and still more who simply bring in a few 1000 very welcome bucks monthly. The concept of producing your own digital product and selling it calls for a little gumption on your part.

- Produce an "ad-supported" blog.

What careers are sought after? - Pay attention to what the market is providing. In a recession there are particular jobs that are required.

Preparing for the Next Great Recession

There are a lot of sites that will send out periodic e-mails with occupation listings. Even if you're not actively looking for fresh or emergency employment, you are able to rapidly view what sorts of positions employers are attempting to fill.

Perfect your tools - While you're between careers, or even if you're lucky to yet be hired during the recession, think about updating your certificates, licenses, and skills. There are a lot of opportunities, from vocational and community college, to volunteer internships and training sessions.

If income is tight, choose to do volunteer work for a non-profit-making organization. This serves 2 purposes: you are able to learn the rudimentary tasks you previously didn't understand how to do, and it lets you socialize and network with a variety of individuals who might know employers that may utilize your tools, or be employers seeking somebody just like you.

Network - maintain your social skills too. Net social networks and blogs as well as loved ones and acquaintances offer personal support while you're looking for work as well as supply contacts and occupation leads.

Recession-Proof Careers

Whenever you've been dismissed and have to find a new line of work, or you're fresh to the job market, barely out of school, or choosing a career, and you aren't sure how long the recession and its residuary effects will last, there are a few fairly "recession-proof" jobs you are able to investigate and/or pick out that have a greater than average chance of pulling through.

Recession-proof careers are those that carry on being required.

Emily Watson

Healthcare is among the quickest growing career areas. Half of the quickest growing jobs are in the healthcare sphere. This includes health services (i.e.: Doctors' helpers and physiotherapists) and home health assistants.

Education is moderately recession-proof. Do your preparation on certain demographic statistics for several geographic areas.

Power is a basic global economic concern. It's come to the forefront in many political elections. Careers related to alternate power, oil, gas, and nuclear sources ought to see stronger emergence in the approaching years.

Global warming is likewise a chief worry among countries. The environmental sphere is a huge and aggressive industry. Not only will professionals with skills in sustainability events be desired through the end of the decade, we're likely to see deficits of pros with 'green' skills.

International occupation supplies a recession-proof vocation if you have a firm and useable cognition of other cultures and languages, and give the sack work in a different country. You'll be in especially high demand if you're "first-generation Chinese" with the power to communicate in Chinese and with applicatory business skills.

Law-breaking doesn't know recession. If anything, stress and pressures induced by a recession may contribute to a growth. Policemen, port security police, and international experts will go on to be required.

PC/IT/Web Development jobs and industry require employees. If you've these tools, you are a blistering commodity! If you're seeking a fresh vocation or training that will get you back into the work force, these are fields that have a good deal to provide.

Preparing for the Next Great Recession

Discovering stable work with great pay might commonly be more of a challenge for those without a higher education, but that's not inevitably the case in a downswing when semi-skilled and unskilled work may be in demand.

Those who press themselves onward and are less meticulous tend to do the best in this time.

Electricians and auto-mechanics (frequently do require skills training)

Hospitality (hotels, motels, and eating places)

Retail

Health, medical, and dental (supporters and clerks)

Chapter 8 – What Investments are Safe from Recession?

Accounts of doomsday and gloom become so commonplace; we sooner or later tune them out. And when we awake one day to gigantic layoffs, explosive markets, and perpetual economic news of global failures and crises, it's too late. By then, all we may do is harm control. All the same, if it's never too late to proactively ready by returning the basics.

With so much talk of a slumping economic system and a down sliding stock market it's difficult to envisage grasping onto any hope of bearing a profit during these times. This section will suggest some hints that might help you survive during an approaching recession.

Choose companies with low debt, firm growth, and solid earnings. In order to choose the better stock from a list of firm companies, pick the one that's farthest from its l week high. This is known as Value Investing.

Preparing for the Next Great Recession

A lot of the country's most affluent entities made their income from snapping bargained stocks and holding on to them till the market healed. If you're able to leave your investitures to grow over a five to ten year period, it's pretty likely that you'll earn an adequate profit. You merely need to search for well-founded companies that are certain to be around and unchanging in the following five to ten years. Consider companies like Coke, GE Electric, P&G, and others.

Split your buying throughout the year. Don't utilize all of your investing income to take over as many shares as you are able to at former. In a recession, stocks are most probable to go on decreasing in price. By the finish of the year, you'll have more stocks for your revenue than if you'd have bought them all together.

Look toward industries that flourish regardless how the economic system is doing. Individuals forever have to eat. Individuals forever require home supplies, even if they aren't spending as much on them. They forever require utilities. Invest in these companies.

Obtain underpriced stocks of a company that's calculated to flourish during a recession. These will be companies that supply a product or service that's "required" instead of "wanted".

Likewise, as individuals spend less income during a recession and commonly hesitate to put out hard cash for large luxury particulars, they'll more than likely spend on add-ons for the items they already have. This may include video games, digital camera elements, mp3 player add-ons, and so forth. Look to invest in these sorts of companies.

Emily Watson
Apply these hints and utilize sound judgments prior to jumping into any investment, your funds ought to start to show promising growth and security in this precarious economic time.

Chapter 9 – How to Bring More Sales to Your Business during Recession

Are you questioning simply how to bring in income in a recession? Whether you're freelance, work for a small business or part of a big corporation, there are a few fundamental principles that will help you endure a recession and even benefit from one. While income is closer during a recession, there's still income to be made if you understand how. Even if you have an unchanging job, it's judicious to seek a secondary source of revenue to supply for expanded expenses and add to your fiscal security. Here's how to bring in income in a recession.

Be originative. Break down your business, products, or business duties. Think about how they may be tweaked to get more demand in an economic recession. You are able to bring in income if you discover a way to provide more value to your wares or services as a small-scale business owner.

Emily Watson

If you're an employee, get invaluable to your company to keep your occupation and even get a raise in spite of the economic down-turn.

Preserve professional and personal relationships, being particularly cautious to effectively communicate with your occupation contacts.

Discover what your customers' requirements are and react to their concerns. Individuals still spend income during a recession; they're simply more measured about it. Acquire the contract by meeting the other person's needs and following up on contacts.

These contacts will likewise prove priceless if you begin a side business or establish a new vocation throughout or after the recession.

Promote bargains or discounts without countermining the value of what you stand for. Focus on the advantages of what you provide, and communicate them to your customers. Rather than dropping the cost, step-up the value of your products or services and convey that to your buyers.

Be an enterpriser. Begin a small home business unofficially to diversify your money sources. Throughout an economic recession, seek a profitable niche by providing crucial goods or services, or bestowing value to existing products.

For instance, a housecleaning service may point out the advantages of house cleaning to customers: time saved on housecleaning allows them more time to be with loved ones or increase their revenue with additional working hours.

Preparing for the Next Great Recession

Assist others survive the economic down-turn, and make income at the same time. For instance, individuals tend to fix appliances and things like bikes instead of replace them when income is tight. Make the best of this truth (for instance) by providing your services as a repair man or beginning a site about do-it-yourself repairs and projects.

Formulate and maximize residual income flows and passive income possibilities to bring in revenue in a recession that will carry on in a great economy, too. You simply have so many hours in the day, so work that will carry on to produce money day-and-night is a great insurance policy.

Whether your passive money comes from originative work (books, info products, net content, and music royalties) or a business or endeavor you found and have running on automatic pilot, you're seeking something that one of these days takes a minimum of day-to-day involvement to carry on generating money.

About The Author

Emily Watson is a writer and a businesswoman. She specializes in finance and money stories primarily because she understands these issues well. She holds a degree in economics.

Emily was born into a family of doctors on March 10, 1965. She has three older sisters, two of whom are doctors while the other is a medical technologist. From an early age, Emily has always wanted to be different. She was not into science like her sisters. She was more interested in the financial section of the Sunday paper.

www.ingramcontent.com/pod-product-compliance
Lightning Source LLC
Chambersburg PA
CBHW070841220526
45466CB00002B/844